THE BODICE BOOK

A WORKBOOK ON PERIOD BODICES

Bonnie Holt Ambrose

Costume & Fashion Press
an imprint of
Quite Specific Media Group Ltd.
New York

email: info@quitespecificmedia.com

Voice: 212.725.5377
Fax: 212.725.8506

The Little Hatmaking Book and The Little Bodice Book were originally published by Drama Publishers

Quite Specific Media Group Ltd. imprints include:

Drama Publishers
Costume & Fashion Press
EntertainmentPro
By Design Press
Jade Rabbit

Printed in Canada

MATERIALS

MUSLIN, BROWN PAPER, TRU-GRID FABRIC, PLASTIC BONING, METAL BONING, BIAS TAPE, COTTON CORDING, ¼" FLEECE LINING, MEDIUM WEIGHT PELLON, METALLIC THREAD, ELASTIC

TOOLS

SCISSORS, IRON, SEWING MACHINE, ZIPPER FOOT ATTACHMENT, #16 SEWING MACHINE NEEDLES, SERGER, STRAIGHT PINS, TAPE MEASURE, GROMMETS, HOLE PUNCH, GROMMET SETTER, HOOKS AND EYES, TAILOR'S HAM

Bodice building continues to be a challenge for me. The method illustrated in this week I learned by altering Stage Costumes from New York, London & Paris. The reward can be a strong, detailed bodice that will last for years.

Bonnie Holt Ambrose

PATTERN MAKING

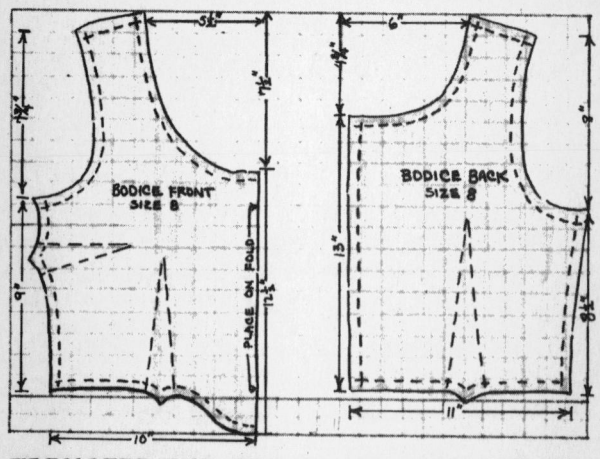

TRANSFER THE BODICE PATTERN ABOVE
TO 1" GRID PAPER. CAREFULLY FOLLOW
MEASUREMENTS AND DRAW ALL DIRECTIONS
ONTO THE PATTERN PIECES WITH A FELT
PEN. IF A DIFFERENT SIZE BODICE IS
DESIRED SEE THE CHART AT THE BACK
OF THE BOOK.
NOW YOU ARE READY TO CUT THE FABRIC
BODICE PIECES. USE PRE-WASHED AND
PRESSED COTTON MUSLIN FOR THE DOUBLE
LINING. CUT 2 BODICE FRONTS ON THE
FOLD AND 4 BODICE BACKS. NOW PLACE
PATTERN PIECES ON THE EXTERIOR FABRIC
AND CUT 1 BODICE FRONT AND 2 BODICE
BACKS.

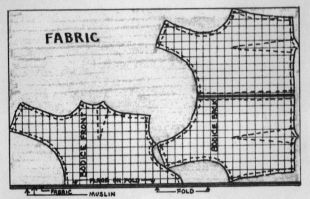

CAREFULLY CONSERVE EXTRA FABRIC FOR
SLEEVES, SKIRT AND BIAS TAPE.

FOLLOW MEASUREMENTS AND DIAGRAMS
ON THE NEXT PAGE FOR PLACEMENT OF
BONING. THE DIAGRAMS ILLUSTRATE
SIMPLE BONING PLACEMENT AND A
MORE EXTENSIVE BONING TREATMENT.
THE PERIOD AND CORSETED LOOK
NEEDED FOR THE BODICE, WILL GOVERN
THE AMOUNT OF BONING NECESSARY.

USE A DARK PENCIL TO MARK WHERE
DARTS AND BONING WILL BE SEWN ON
ONE OF THE MUSLIN LININGS. USE ONE
MUSLIN LINING FOR A FITTING. BASTE
OR PIN TOGETHER SHOULDER AND SIDE
SEAMS. PIN IN DARTS. FIT MUSLIN
BODICE TO WEARER AND ADJUST DARTS
AND SIDE SEAMS ACCORDINGLY.

SIMPLE BONING

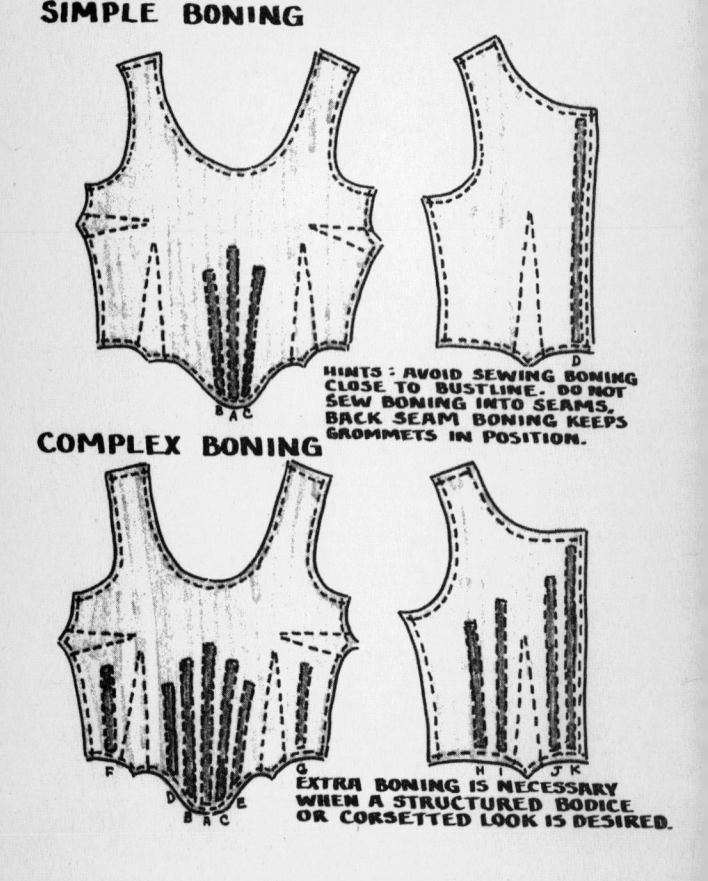

HINTS: AVOID SEWING BONING CLOSE TO BUSTLINE. DO NOT SEW BONING INTO SEAMS. BACK SEAM BONING KEEPS GROMMETS IN POSITION.

COMPLEX BONING

EXTRA BONING IS NECESSARY WHEN A STRUCTURED BODICE OR CORSETTED LOOK IS DESIRED.

BODICE BONING

BEGIN THIS STEP WITH THE 2 PRE-MARKED
FRONT MUSLIN LININGS. PIN THEM
TOGETHER AT VARIOUS PLACES LEAVING
THE WAIST AREA OPEN.

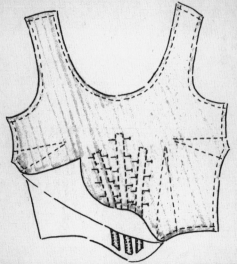

MEASURE LENGTH OF BONING PIECES TO
BE USED. CUT AND IRON BONING FLAT.
SANDWICH BONING BETWEEN MUSLIN
LAYERS AND SECURE BY PINNING.
FOLLOW THE SAME PROCEDURE FOR
BACK BODICE.

SET SEWING MACHINE
FOOT DIRECTLY DOWN
ON BONING, STITCH
CAREFULLY AT THE
EDGE OF THE BONING
COMPLETELY BOXING
IT IN. AVOID NEEDLE
AND BONING CONTACT.
BONING SHOULD NOT
RUN INTO SEAM OR
DART LINES. BE SURE
TO LEAVE A ½"
CLEARANCE IN THESE
AREAS.
AFTER INSERTING AND SEWING BONING
IN BODICE FRONT AND BACK, THE OUTER

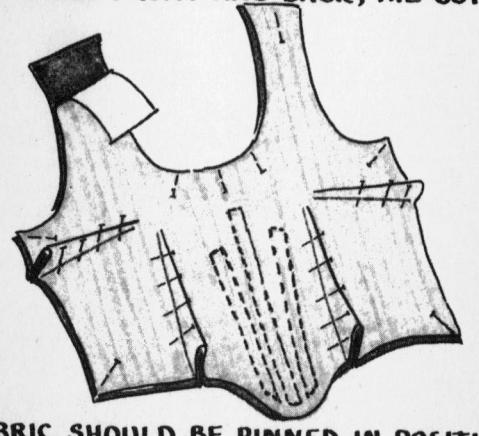

FABRIC SHOULD BE PINNED IN POSITION.
PIN DARTS AS MARKED THRU ALL
LAYERS OF FABRICS.

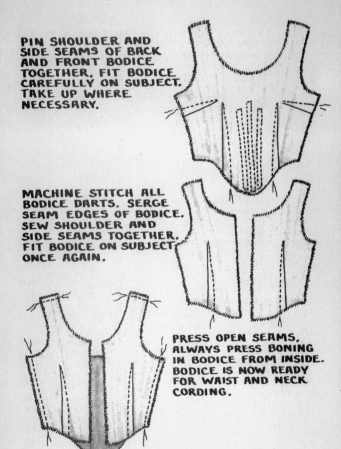

PIN SHOULDER AND
SIDE SEAMS OF BACK
AND FRONT BODICE
TOGETHER, FIT BODICE
CAREFULLY ON SUBJECT.
TAKE UP WHERE
NECESSARY.

MACHINE STITCH ALL
BODICE DARTS. SERGE
SEAM EDGES OF BODICE.
SEW SHOULDER AND
SIDE SEAMS TOGETHER.
FIT BODICE ON SUBJECT
ONCE AGAIN.

PRESS OPEN SEAMS,
ALWAYS PRESS BONING
IN BODICE FROM INSIDE.
BODICE IS NOW READY
FOR WAIST AND NECK
CORDING.

CORDING

CORDING USED AT THE NECKLINE AND
WAIST OF THE BODICE MAKES A NICE
FINISHED EDGE AND OUTLINES THESE
AREAS. USE A DARKER OR COMPLIMENTARY
COLOR. COVERED CORDING CAN BE
PURCHASED, HOWEVER THE FOLLOWING
STEPS WILL SHOW YOU HOW TO MAKE
YOUR OWN.

CUT 1½" TO 2" BIAS STRIPS AND SEW
TOGETHER IN NECESSARY LENGTHS FOR
NECKLINE AND WAISTLINE.
FOLD BIAS OVER CORDING AS SHOWN BELOW.
USE ZIPPER FOOT ATTACHMENT TO
STITCH CORDING SNUGLY INTO BIAS TAPE.

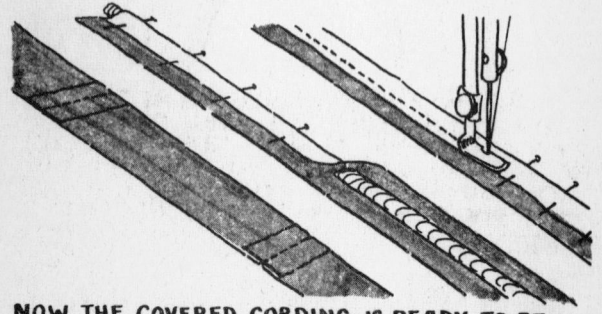

NOW THE COVERED CORDING IS READY TO BE
PINNED INTO THE BODICE NECKLINE. WITH
THE GOOD SIDE OF THE CORDING UP, PIN
THE CORDING TO THE OUTSIDE NECKLINE
EDGE. STITCH THE CORDING IN POSITION.
USE A ZIPPER FOOT AND FOLLOW THE
ORIGINAL STITCHING THREADS AS A GUIDE.
SEE ILLUSTRATIONS ON THE NEXT PAGE.

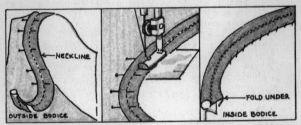

CLIP AROUND CURVED NECKLINE SEAM BUT
AVOID CLIPPING BIAS CORDING FABRIC AS
THIS BECOMES THE BIAS TAPE TO FINISH OFF
THE NECKLINE. PRESS DOWN BIAS EDGE
OF CORDING TAPE AND FOLD UNDER ¼".
PIN BIAS IN POSITION AND SLIP STITCH.

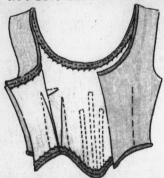

ONE OF THE MOST IMPORTANT DETAILS
FOR STAGE BODICES IS <u>OUTLINING</u>. CORDING
AT THE WAIST AND NECK NOT ONLY FINISHES
THE BODICE BEAUTIFULLY AND STRENGTHENS
IT BUT OUTLINES IT VISUALLY FOR THE
AUDIENCE.

GROMMETS

USING GROMMETS AS A CLOSURE ALLOWS YOU TO ADJUST A BODICE UP TO THREE SIZES. IT GIVES AN AUTHENTIC LOOK OF LACING WITH A SMOOTH TIGHT FIT AND ELIMINATES THE CHANCE OF BROKEN ZIPPERS.

BODICE BACK

BONING

BONING SHOULD BE INSERTED AT FOLD ON BOTH SIDES OF THE BACK CLOSURE. SECURE BONING BY MACHINE STITCHING ALONG INSIDE EDGE. THE BONING SUPPORTS PRESSURE EXERTED ON GROMMETS FROM TIGHT LACING.

MARK SPACING FOR GROMMETS AT 2" APART. CUT HOLES WITH HOLE PUNCH AND HAMMER. WORK ON TOP OF SCRAP LUMBER SO AS NOT TO DULL HOLE PUNCH OR MAR TABLE SURFACE. ½" BRASS GROMMETS ARE SUGGESTED. FOLLOW INSTRUCTIONS ON GROMMET PACKAGE TO SET UPPER AND LOWER GROMMET PARTS.

BACK PLACKET
THE BACK PLACKET, GROMMETS AND LACING MAKE THE BODICE ADJUSTABLE IN SIZE.

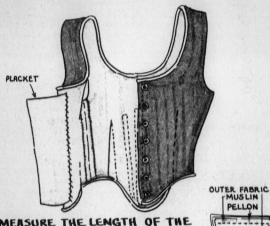

PLACKET

OUTER FABRIC
MUSLIN
PELLON

MEASURE THE LENGTH OF THE BODICE OPENING AND CUT THE PLACKET ACCORDINGLY. CUT 3 LAYERS OF FABRIC: 1 OUTER FABRIC, 1 MUSLIN LINING, AND 1 PELLON. POSITION FABRICS AS SHOWN IN THE ILLUSTRATION. SEW ON 3 SIDES, TURN AND PRESS. SERGE THE REMAINING SIDE, BASTE INTO BODICE CLOSURE AS SHOWN ABOVE. SOMETIMES BY JUST MAKING ANOTHER LARGER PLACKET THE BODICE CAN INCREASE TWO OR THREE SIZES.

SLEEVE PATTERN

TRANSFER THIS SLEEVE PATTERN TO 1" GRID PAPER OR BROWN PAPER. CUT OUT THE SLEEVE PATTERN AND USE A FELT PEN TO TRANSFER ALL SEAMS, DARTS AND DIRECTIONS. IF ANOTHER SIZE IS DESIRED REFER TO THE SIZE CHART AT THE BACK OF THE BOOK. NOTICE THE ANGLE OF THE SLEEVE TOP. CUTTING THE SLEEVE WITH LESS OF A CONFINING ANGLE WILL ENABLE THE WEARER MORE FREEDOM OF MOVEMENT.

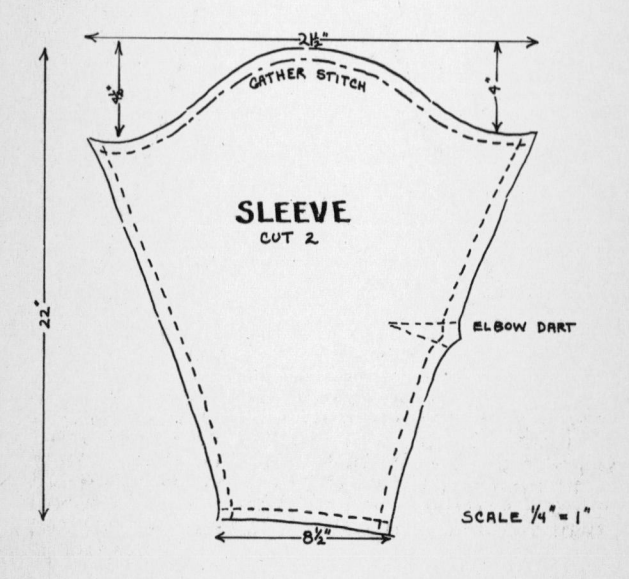

GATHER STITCH

2½"

3"

4"

22"

SLEEVE
CUT 2

ELBOW DART

8½"

SCALE ¼" = 1"

SLEEVE

USE SLEEVE PATTERN TO CUT SLEEVES AND
LININGS. THE FABRIC FOR LININGS SHOULD
BE MUSLIN OR A LIGHT WEIGHT COTTON.
PLACE ONE SLEEVE FABRIC AND A LINING
TOGETHER AND SERGE ALL EDGES. SEW
A GATHERING STITCH ACROSS TOP OF THE
SLEEVE. SEW IN ELBOW DART.

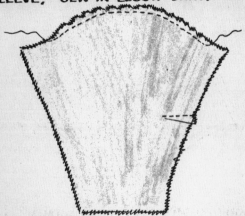

EASE THE TOP GATHERING STITCH. SEW IN
THE UNDER ARM SLEEVE SEAM. PRESS
THE SEAM OPEN.

TURN THE SLEEVE RIGHT SIDE OUT AND
CAREFULLY PIN IT INTO THE ARMEYE.
BE SURE THE ELBOW DART IS POINTING
TOWARD THE BODICE BACK. STITCH
SLEEVE INTO ARMEYE.

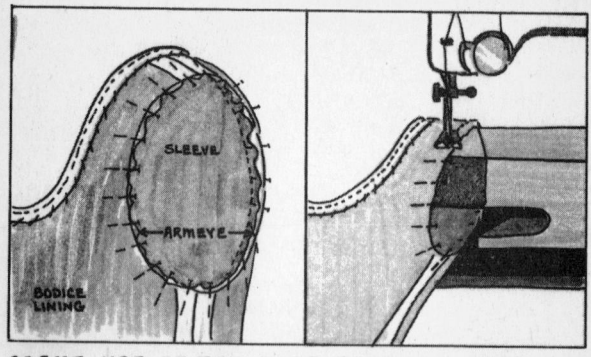

MAKE USE OF THE FREE ARM ON YOUR
MACHINE TO SEW AROUND THE ARMEYE.
TURN SLEEVES RIGHT SIDE OUT AND STEAM
PRESS. USE A TAILOR'S HAM IF AVAILABLE.
PRESS BODICE THROUGHOUT SEWING
PROCESS. TO AVOID MARKING OUTSIDE
FABRIC ALWAYS PRESS BODICE BONING
FROM THE INSIDE.

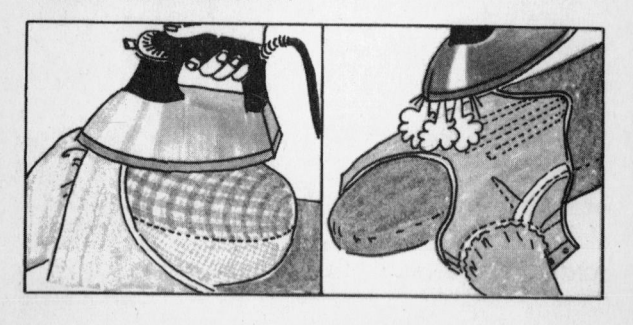

TO FINISH OFF THE BOTTOM EDGE OF THE
SLEEVE, OPEN THE LAST 3" OF THE UNDER-
ARM SEAM AT THE WRIST. SECURE THE
OPENING WITH A TACK STITCH. MACHINE
STITCH BIAS TAPE ON SLEEVE AT WRIST
EDGE, TURN BIAS TAPE TO INSIDE, PRESS
AND PIN. HEM STITCH WRIST OPENING
AND BIAS TAPE, ADD SNAP, HOOK & EYE,
OR BUTTON FOR CLOSURE AT WRIST.

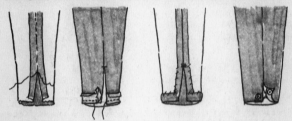

THE TREATMENT OF SLEEVE DESIGN AND CUT
IS LIMITLESS. A FEW FINISHES FOR THE
WRIST ON A LONG, STRAIGHT SLEEVE
ARE SHOWN BELOW.

SAME BODICE, DIFFERENT TRIM

CHANGING THE TRIM WILL CHANGE THE
ATTITUDE, STYLE AND PERIOD OF THE
GARMENT.

INORDER TO RE-DECORATE EASILY, SEW
THE TRIM ON AFTER ALL CONSTRUCTION
IS FINISHED ON THE BODICE.

THE VICTORIAN BODICE

THE VICTORIAN LOOK CAN BE ACHIEVED BY ADDING A HIGH NECK INSET, A LEG-O-MUTTON SLEEVE AND EXTRA TRIM.

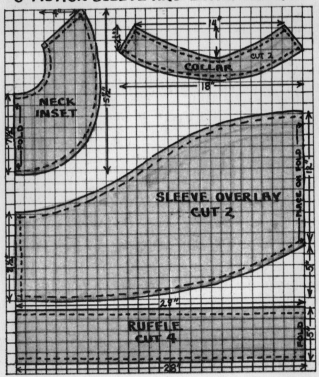

COLLAR
CUT 2

NECK INSET

SLEEVE OVERLAY
CUT 2

PLACE ON FOLD

RUFFLE
CUT 4

FOLLOW THE PATTERN GUIDE ON THE PRECEEDING PAGE. USE TRUE-GRID FABRIC OR BROWN PAPER FOR YOUR PATTERN PIECES. CHOOSE A CRISP FABRIC FOR THE SLEEVES AND RUFFLES. CUT ALL PATTERN PIECES PLUS A PELLON INNERFACING FOR THE COLLAR. SERGE THE EDGES OF THE NECK INSET AND THE TOP AND BOTTOM SEAMS OF THE SLEEVE. PRESS THE PELLON ONTO ONE OF THE COLLAR PIECES. MACHINE STITCH SIDES AND TOP SEAM OF COLLAR. TURN AND PRESS. USE A ROLLED HEM ON BOTH SIDES OF NECK INSET BACK SEAM. PIN COLLAR TO NECK INSET PIECE LEAVING ONE SIDE OF THE COLLAR FREE. MACHINE STITCH COLLAR IN PLACE AND FOLD LOOSE COLLAR EDGE UNDER AND WHIP STITCH.

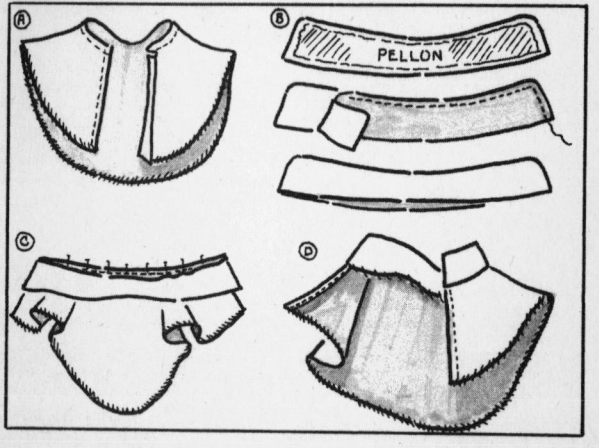

SEW BUTTONS AND LACE TRIM TO COLLAR.
FIT BODICE TO WEARER OR DRESS FORM.
PIN FINISHED NECK INSET INTO BODICE
NECKLINE. REMOVE FROM DRESS FORM
AND WHIP STITCH INSET INTO BODICE.

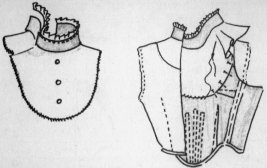

SLEEVE OVERLAY
THE SLEEVE OVERLAY SHOULD ALREADY BE
SERGED AT THE TOP AND LOWER SEAM.
MACHINE STITCH A GATHERING THREAD ½"
IN FROM UPPER AND LOWER SEAMS.

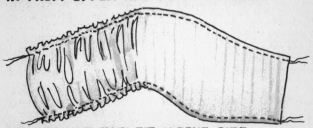

GATHER OVERLAY TO FIT SLEEVE SIZE.

PIN SHEER OVERLAY DIRECTLY TO UPPER
SLEEVE AND MACHINE STITCH IN POSITION.
PIN RIBBON TRIM AS DESIGNED ONTO SLEEVE.
WRIST TRIM SHOULD BE APPLIED AT THIS
TIME. STITCH TRIM IN POSITION.

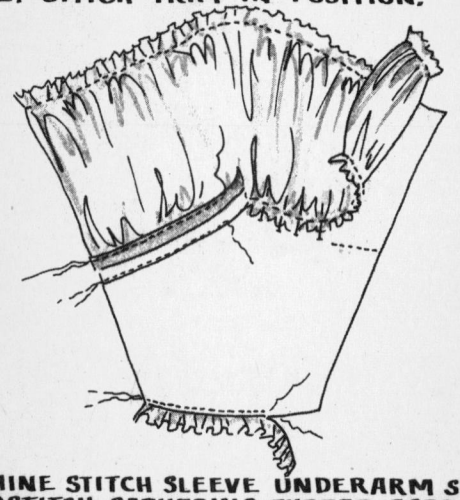

MACHINE STITCH SLEEVE UNDERARM SEAM.
HANDSTITCH GATHERING THREAD ACROSS
TOP OF SLEEVE, EASE AND PIN INTO ARMEYE.
MACHINE STITCH SLEEVE INTO BODICE.
LEAVE THE LAST 3" OF UNDERARM SEAM
OPEN FOR A WRIST PLACKET. ADD HOOK
AND EYE FOR THIS CLOSURE. BUTTONS
CAN BE USED AS TRIM ON SLEEVE PLACKET.
HAND TACK BOWS TO CENTER OF SLEEVE
TRIM.

RUFFLES

SEW THE RUFFLE PIECES TOGETHER.
MACHINE STITCH A ROLL HEM ON LOWER
EDGE OF RUFFLE. GATHER STITCH ACROSS
TOP EDGE OF RUFFLE. ADD ANY LACE OR
RIBBON TRIM AT THIS POINT.

PULL GATHERING THREAD TO DESIRED FULLNESS.
PIN RUFFLES ONTO BODICE NECKLINE.
POSITION LEFT-OVER RUFFLES ACROSS
SLEEVE TOP. FINISH END SEAMS WITH A
ROLL HEM. HAND STITCH RUFFLE TRIM
ONTO BODICE.

ROCOCO - 1770
ADAPTATIONS OF THE SAME BODICE

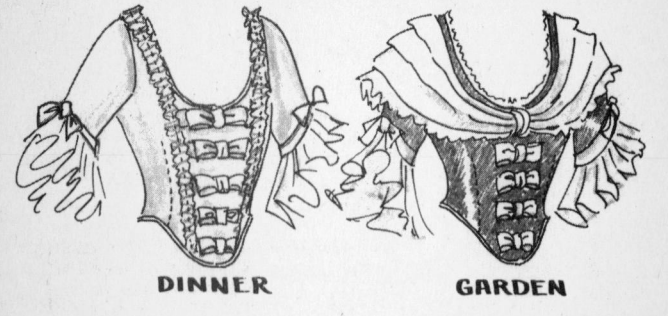

DINNER   GARDEN

TRAVEL    PARTY

ATTACHING TRIM

USE 1½" SATIN OR VELVET RIBBON. THE TOP BOW SHOULD BE CUT 15" LONG AND FOLDED AS IN THE ILLUSTRATION. EACH SUCCESSIVE BOW SHOULD BE CUT 2" SHORTER.

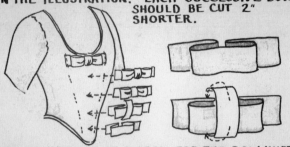

CUT A 2¼" PIECE OF RIBBON FOR THE BOW KNOT. WRAP RIBBON AROUND THE CENTER OF FOLDED BOW AND TACK STITCH. STITCH BOWS TO BODICE AS SHOWN ABOVE. MAKE BOX-PLEATED RUFFLES OUT OF 1¼" RIBBON. PIN PLEATS INTO RIBBON AND MACHINE STITCH DOWN. HAND-SEW RUFFLES TO BODICE.

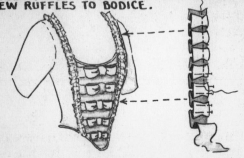

TO ADD A SHEER CIRCULAR CUT RUFFLE AND
A HANDMADE BOW TO THE ELBOW LENGTH
SLEEVE FOLLOW THIS GRID AND CUT YOUR
OWN PATTERN.

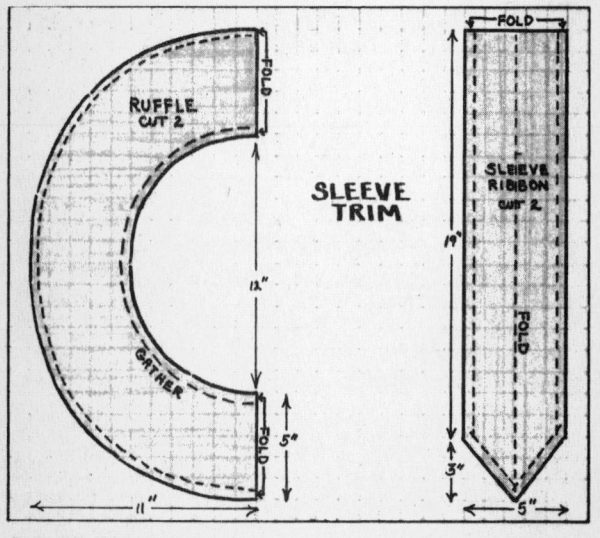

PLACE RUFFLE PATTERN ON FOLD OF SHEER
FABRIC AND CUT TWO. HEM RUFFLE EDGE
BY USING OVER-CAST STITCH OF SERGER
OR BY USING A ROLL HEM DONE WITH THE
SEWING MACHINE. ADD GATHERING STITCH
TO INNER CIRCLE AND PULL GATHERING
THREADS TO FIT LOWER EDGE OF SLEEVE.
PIN RUFFLE TO SLEEVE AT LOWER EDGE.

FOLD RIBBON DOWN CENTER. STITCH SEAM
LEAVING A 3" OPENING NEAR CENTER. TURN
RIBBON BY PULLING ENDS THRU CENTER
OPENING. PRESS. SLIP STITCH OPENING
CLOSED. PIN HANDMADE RIBBON TO
SLEEVE AND TACK IN POSITION.

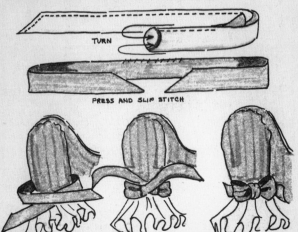

TURN

PRESS AND SLIP STITCH

RESTORATION — 1650
SAME BODICE — DIFFERENT CLASSES

PEASANT

UPPER CLASS

COURT

TRAVEL

RESTORATION COURT BODICE

TRANSFER THE PATTERN PIECES BELOW TO GRID FABRIC OR PAPER. MARK ALL DARTS, SEAMS, AND LABEL PATTERN PIECES. USE A MEDIUM WEIGHT, SHINY FABRIC FOR THE SLEEVE OVERLAY. CUT THE PEPLUM FROM BODICE FABRIC AND LINE WITH A COMPLIMENTARY COLOR. USE WHITE FABRIC FOR THE CUFFS.

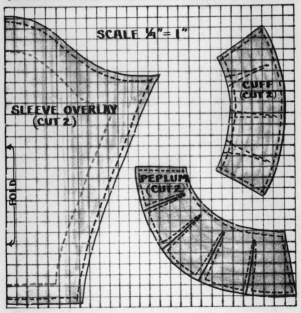

SCALE ¼"= 1"

SLEEVE OVERLAY
(CUT 2.)

FOLD

CUFF
(CUT 2.)

PEPLUM
(CUT 2.)

GATHER TOP AND BOTTOM OF THE OUTER
SLEEVE FABRIC AND PIN THE GATHERED EDGES
TO THE UNDER SLEEVE. SECURE THE TWO
LAYERS BY STITCHING TOP AND BOTTOM SEAMS.

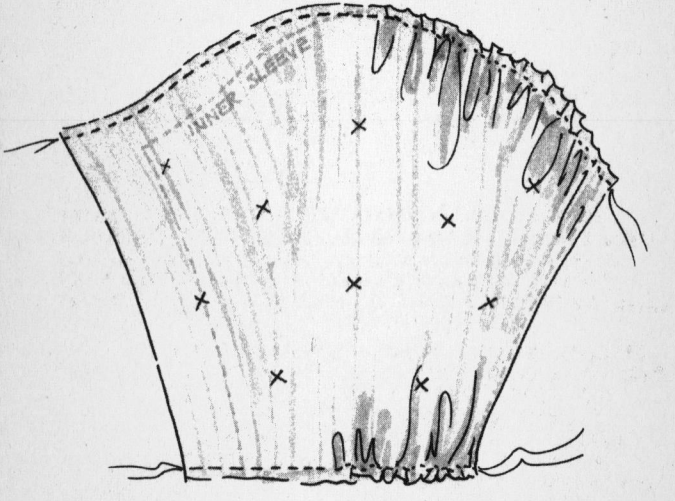

TO ACHEIVE A TUFTED LOOK, TACK STITCH
OUTER SLEEVE AT "X's" TO INNER SLEEVE.
IF EXTRA CRISPNESS IS DESIRED, ADD A
CENTER SLEEVE LAYER OF INNERFACING.
WHILE TACKING SLEEVE AT "X's", JEWELS
OR BUTTONS CAN BE ADDED TO EMPHASIZE
THIS DRAMATIC SLEEVE EFFECT. MACHINE
STITCH UNDERARM SEAM.

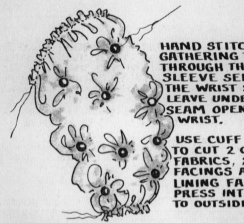

HAND STITCH A GATHERING THREAD THROUGH THE TOP SLEEVE SEAM AND THE WRIST SEAM. LEAVE UNDERARM SEAM OPEN 2½" AT WRIST.

USE CUFF PATTERN TO CUT 2 OUTER FABRICS, 2 INTERFACINGS AND 2 LINING FABRICS. PRESS INTERFACING TO OUTSIDE FABRIC.

MARK DARTS ON OUTER AND LINING FABRIC. MACHINE STITCH DARTS. PLACE RIGHT SIDES OF CUFF PIECES TOGETHER, STITCH OUTSIDE SEAMS, CLIP CORNERS, TURN AND PRESS. STITCH LACE TRIM NEAR TOP EDGE OF CUFF.

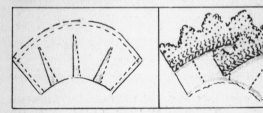

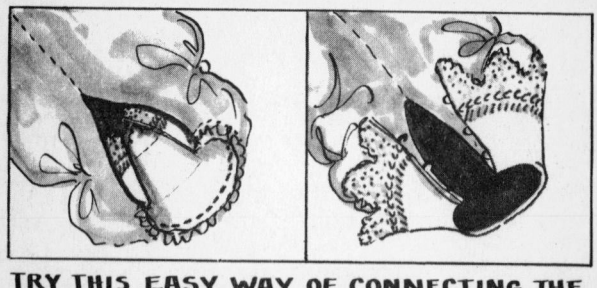

TRY THIS EASY WAY OF CONNECTING THE
CUFF TO A THICK GATHERED SLEEVE. INSERT
THE CUFF INTO THE LOWER SLEEVE OPENING
WITH THE RIGHT SIDE OF THE CUFF FACING
THE WRONG SIDE OF THE SLEEVE, MACHINE
STITCH ALL LAYERS TOGETHER. PULL THE
CUFF OUT OF THE SLEEVE AND FOLD IT UP
INTO POSITION. ADD HOOKS AND EYES TO
CUFF FOR WRIST CLOSURE.

PEPLUM
CUT 2 OUTER FABRIC PIECES, 2 LININGS
AND 2 INTERFACINGS.

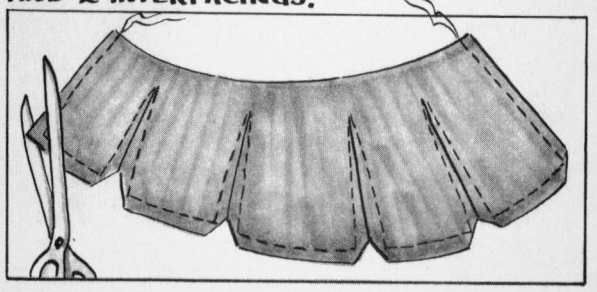

RESTORATION PEASANT BODICE

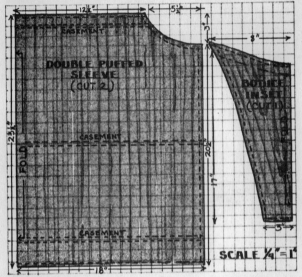

CUT 2 PIECES OF THE DOUBLE PUFFED
SLEEVE PATTERN AND 1 PIECE OF THE
BODICE INSET PATTERN. BOTH PATTERN
PIECES MUST BE PLACED ON THE FOLD.
SUGGESTED FABRIC IS OF LIGHTER WEIGHT
AND A COMPLIMENTARY COLOR. DRAW
CASEMENT LINES ON THE WRONG SIDE
OF SLEEVES WITH A CHALK PENCIL,
SEW A ROLL HEM AT TOP OF SLEEVE
AND ACROSS BOTTOM EDGE.

SEW IN BIAS TAPE FOR CASEMENT AT TOP, MIDDLE, AND BOTTOM OF SLEEVE.

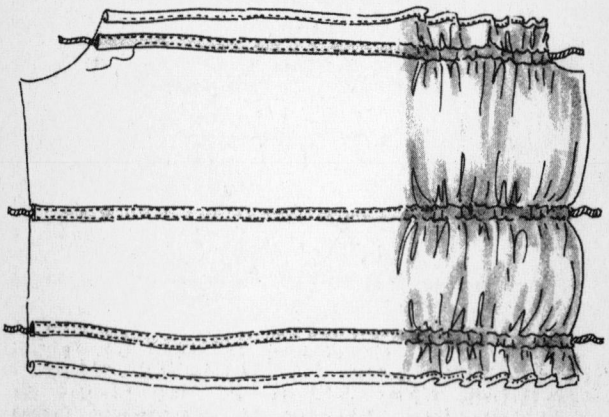

ANY TRIM FOR SLEEVE SHOULD BE ADDED AT THIS TIME.

¼" ELASTIC SHOULD BE INSERTED IN THE CASEMENT. ATTACH A SMALL GOLD SAFETY PIN FOR EASY CASEMENT THREADING. SECURE ELASTIC AT OUTER EDGES AFTER DRAWING UP TO APPROPRIATE SIZE.

FOR A MORE DECORATIVE LOOK, REVERSE CASEMENT TO FRONT OF SLEEVE AND SUBSTITUTE SATIN RIBBON IN A CONTRASTING COLOR. FOLLOW SAME INSTRUCTIONS AS FOR BIAS TAPE. THIS METHOD WILL DEFINE THE SLEEVE MORE EFFECTIVELY.

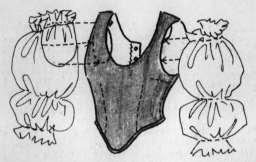

SEW UNDERARM SLEEVE SEAM TOGETHER.
TURN SLEEVE RIGHT SIDE OUT AND PIN
INTO ARMEYE OF BODICE. HANDSTITCH
IN POSITION. SECURELY TACK SHOULDER
ELASTIC AT ARMEYE. BIAS TAPE CAN BE
USED TO FINISH SEAM OF ARMEYE.

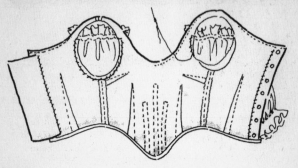

ELIZABETHAN — 1600
SAME BODICE — DIFFERENT CLASSES

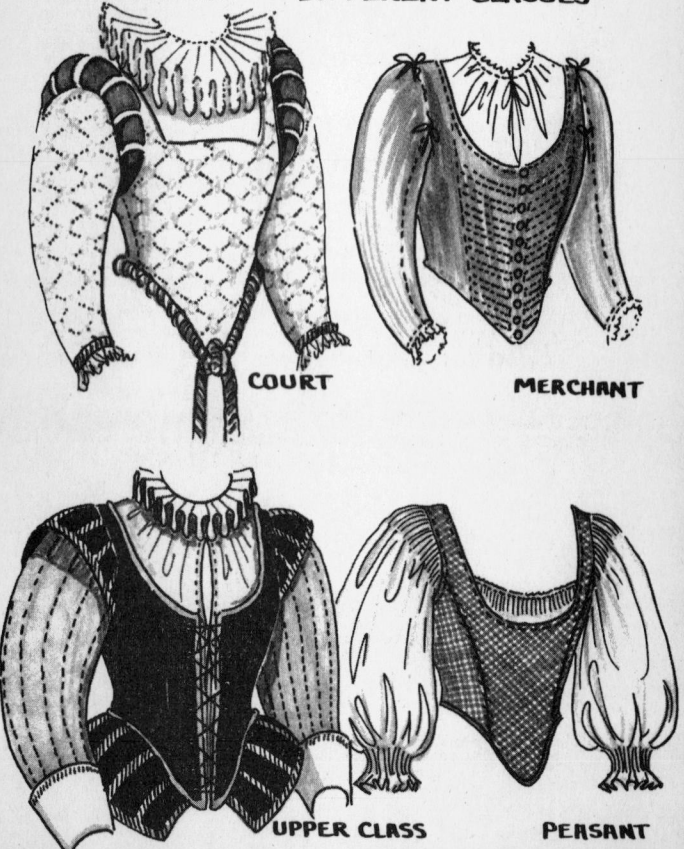

COURT

MERCHANT

UPPER CLASS

PEASANT

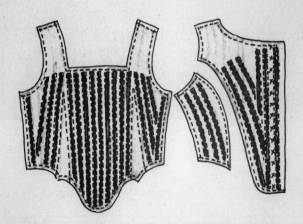

TO BUILD THIS MORE STRUCTURED, FLAT
BODICE USE THE SAME GENERAL BODICE
PATTERN FOUND IN THE FRONT OF THIS
BOOK WITH A FEW ADJUSTMENTS.
REMOVE THE BUST DARTS AND RUN THE
BONING UP TO THE FRONT NECKLINE
SEAM. FOR A MORE AUTHENTIC LOOK
SUBSTITUTE METAL BONING FOR PLASTIC.
SPACE THE BONING ½" APART AND
CAREFULLY AVOID RUNNING INTO SEAMS.
TRY THE DIFFERENT CUT OF THE TWO PIECE
PATTERN AS SHOWN ABOVE FOR THE BODICE
BACK.

15ᵀᴴ–16ᵀᴴ CENTURY SLEEVE TREATMENTS

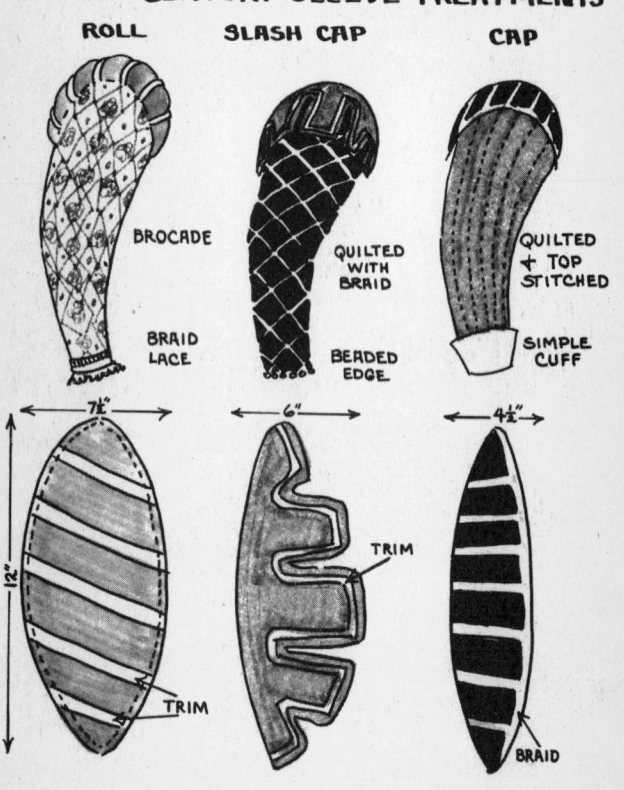

ROLL

BROCADE

BRAID
LACE

SLASH CAP

QUILTED
WITH
BRAID

BEADED
EDGE

CAP

QUILTED
+ TOP
STITCHED

SIMPLE
CUFF

7½"

12"

TRIM

6"

TRIM

4½"

BRAID

QUILTING AS TRIM

CUT AN OUTER FABRIC, FLEECE INNER-LINING, AND A LINING FOR THE THREE LAYERS OF THIS SLEEVE TREATMENT. DRAW SEWING GUIDE LINES FOR QUILTING ON OUTER FABRIC. PIN ALL THREE LAYERS TOGETHER IN PREPARATION FOR SEWING.

DIFFERENT THREADS AND STITCHES CAN BE USED TO DRAMATIZE THIS SLEEVE EFFECT. GOLD OR SILVER METALLIC THREAD SHOULD BE CONSIDERED. PRACTICE WITH DIFFERENT STITCHES ON SCRAP FABRIC. AFTER CHOOSING THE CORRECT STITCH AND THREAD, CAREFULLY PIN THE AREAS TO BE QUILTED. ALWAYS START EACH ROW OF QUILTING FROM THE SAME SIDE. AFTER ALL DECORATIVE STITCHING ON SLEEVE IS FINISHED SERGE SEAM EDGES.

SLEEVE CAPS AND ROLLS

USE MEASUREMENTS ON PRECEDING PAGE FOR PATTERN OF SLASH SLEEVE CAP. CUT TWO OUTER FABRICS AND LININGS. SEW METALLIC BRAID TRIM 3/4" FROM SLASH EDGES. SEW LINING AND OUTER FABRIC TOGETHER AROUND

SLASHED EDGES USING A ¼" SEAM ALLOWANCE.
CLIP INSIDE CORNERS OF SLASHES CAREFULLY.
TURN AND PRESS. FOLD REMAINING SEAM
TO THE INSIDE AND WHIP STITCH CLOSED.

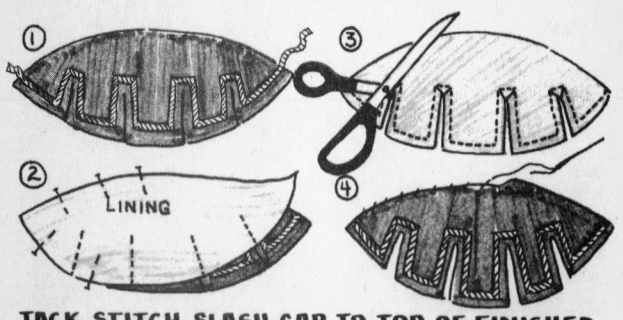

TACK STITCH SLASH CAP TO TOP OF FINISHED
SLEEVE. THE CAP MAY ALSO BE MACHINE
STITCHED INTO THE ARMEYE WHEN THE
SLEEVE IS SEWN INTO THE BODICE.
USE MEASUREMENTS AT THE BEGINNING OF
THIS SECTION TO CUT THE SHOULDER ROLL.
PLACE PATTERN ON BIAS OF FABRIC AND CUT
2 PIECES. APPLY TRIM TO EACH CUT OUT
ROLL. PIN OR BASTE SHOULDER ROLL CLOSED.

LEAVE 3" OPEN FOR INSERTING STUFFING.
STUFF ROLL WITH COTTON BATTING OR FIBER-
FILL. WHIP STITCH ENTIRE SEAM CLOSED
AND TACK TO SHOULDER SEAM.

A SLASHED TRIM CAN BE ADDED TO THE
BODICE TO GIVE A RENAISSANCE LOOK.
SLASH TRIM IS MADE BY CUTTING A 6"
WIDE BY 14" LONG LIGHT-WEIGHT FABRIC.

FOLD THE FABRIC IN HALF, LENGTHWISE
AND SEAM. TURN RIGHT SIDE OUT AND
PRESS. GATHER ACROSS SHEER TUBE AT
3" INTERVALS. POSITION PUFFED TRIM ON
BODICE AS SHOWN. TACK DOWN PUFFS
WITH BUTTON OR RIBBON TRIM. A 2" WIDE
RIBBON CROSSING THE BODICE ABOVE THE
BUSTLINE FINISHES THE LOOK. AN 18"
PIECE OF METALLIC BROCADE RIBBON
WILL SET OFF A RICH VELVET OR BROCADE
BODICE AND SLEEVES.

JOINING BODICE TO SKIRT

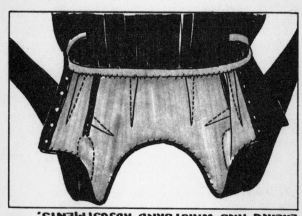

BUILDING THE BODICE INDEPENDANT OF THE SKIRT ALLOWS FOR A MORE STRUCTURED BODICE, HEAVY PLEATING OR GATHERS AT WAISTLINE, AND EASY REMOVAL FOR CLEANING OR REPLACEMENT.

USE 1"GROSGRAIN FOR WAISTBAND. MEASURE AND CUT RIBBON 6" LONGER THAN WAIST LENGTH. PIN PLEATED OR GATHERED SKIRT ONTO WAIST-BAND. INSERT A 4"WIDE BY 11"LONG PLACKET AT BACK SKIRT SEAM. MACHINE STITCH. HAND STITCH GROSGRAIN WAISTBAND AND SKIRT TO BODICE AT WAISTLINE. USE BUTTONHOLE TWIST FOR STRENGTH. AVOID SEWING THRU TO THE OUTSIDE BODICE FABRIC. CONCENTRATE STITCHES ON TOP OF DARTS AND SEAMS. STITCH WAISTBAND TO BODICE FROM BACK DART TO BACK DART ONLY. THIS ALLOWS FOR EASIER LACING AND WAISTBAND ADJUSTMENTS.

BODICE MEASUREMENTS

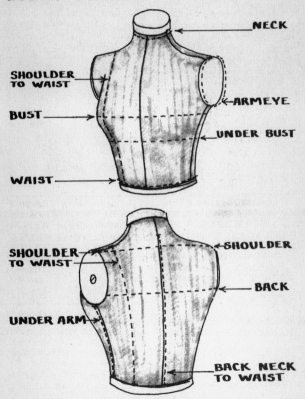

NECK

SHOULDER
TO WAIST

ARMEYE

BUST

UNDER BUST

WAIST

SHOULDER
TO WAIST

SHOULDER

BACK

UNDER ARM

BACK NECK
TO WAIST

SIZE CONVERSION CHART

THE MEASUREMENTS BELOW ARE APPROXIMATE.

SIZE	BUST	WAIST	UNDER BUST	SHOULDER	NECK	NECK TO WAIST	ARMHOLE	SLEEVE
6	32	25	29	14½	12½	15	16	29
8	34	26	30	15	13	16	17	30
10	36	27	32	15½	13½	17	18	30½
12	38	29	33	16	14	18	19	31
14	40	31	34	16	14½	18½	20	31
16	42	33	36	16½	15	19	21	31½
18	44	35	37	17	15½	19½	22	32
20	46	37	39	17½	16	20	23	33

MEASURE YOUR SUBJECT CAREFULLY.

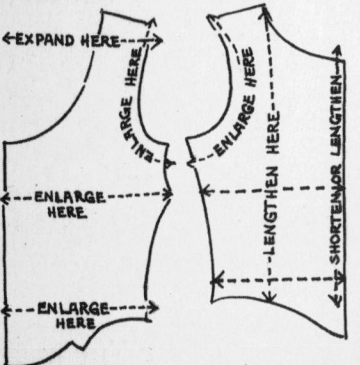

←EXPAND HERE→

ENLARGE HERE

←ENLARGE HERE→

←ENLARGE HERE

ENLARGE HERE

ENLARGE HERE→

LENGTHEN HERE

LENGTHEN HERE

←SHORTEN OR LENGTHEN→

ADJUST YOUR PAPER PATTERN AS SHOWN ABOVE.

ALSO AVAILABLE IN THIS SERIES:

THE LITTLE HATMAKING BOOK

EASY TO FOLLOW GUIDE ON THE CONSTRUCTION OF
A LARGE BRIM TURN-OF-THE-CENTURY HAT FRAME.
PATTERNS, COVERING AND TRIMMING TECHNIQUES
SHOWN.

THE LITTLE CORSET BOOK

CORSET BUILDING MADE EASY. STEP-BY-STEP
INSTRUCTION FOR PRODUCING A DIFFICULT COSTUME
UNDERGARMENT.

SOON TO BE PUBLISHED:
THE LITTLE HATMAKING BOOK II

AN EASY TO FOLLOW GUIDE ON BUILDING ELIZABETHAN,
TUDOR AND RENAISSANCE HATS FOR MEN AND WOMEN.

ALSO AVAILABLE:

THE COSTUME WORKSHOP

A 'HOW-TO' TELEVISION SERIES DEMONSTRATING EASY
AND ECONOMICAL METHODS OF BUILDING COSTUMES.
THESE SHOWS ARE AVAILABLE IN 30 MINUTE V.H.S.

SHOW #1....LARGE BRIM VICTORIAN HAT FRAME
           CONSTRUCTION.
SHOW #2...COVERING AND TRIMMING A VICTORIAN
           HAT.
SHOW #3...FROM GARAGE SALE TO RENAISSANCE
           COSTUME.
SHOW #4...BUILDING A TURN-OF-THE-CENTURY CAPE
           AND SKIRT THE EASY WAY.
SHOW #5...FROM RESALE TO VICTORIAN WEDDING
           DRESS.
SHOW #6...AN "1830" UNIFORM COAT FROM A NAVY

BLUE BLAZER.
SHOW #7...TRIMMING THE VICTORIAN WEDDING DRESS
FROM SHOW 5.
SHOW #8...A SMALL BOY'S KNIGHT COSTUME THE
EASY WAY.
SHOW #9...BUILDING LIGHT WEIGHT MEDIEVAL
CROWNS.
SHOW #10..CONSTRUCTING AN INNVERNESS CAPE
WITHOUT A PATTERN.

FOR A FREE BROCHURE AND FURTHER INFORMATION
CONTACT:

BONNIE HOLT AMBROSE
THE COSTUME WORKSHOP
417 REINICKE
HOUSTON, TEXAS 77007
1 (713) 864-3969